Tiny Courts
in a world without scales

Tiny Courts
in a world without scales

David Bromige

Brick Books

CANADIAN CATALOGUING
IN PUBLICATION DATA

Bromige, David
    Tiny courts in a world without scales

Poems.
ISBN 0-919626-53-X

I. Title.

PS3552.R65T5 1991   811'.54   C91-095574-3

The support of The Canada Council and the
Ontario Arts Council is gratefully acknowledged
by Brick Books.

Thanks to *A Stone's Throw*, *The Carleton Literary
Review*, *Loose Gravel*, *Screens and Tasted
Parallels*, *Slug Press*, *Talisman*, and *Tomcat*.

Printed on Zephyr Antique Laid, sewn into
signatures and bound by The Porcupine's Quill,
Inc., Erin, Ontario.

Brick Books
Box 38, Station B
London, Ontario
N6A 4V3

Contents

for anselm hollo

let's not have the finnish
for *il miglior fabbro*

The state supplanted gold

'Irony' i read
but it said 'Money'

Community leaders

The county assessor
likes to drink with mr. tom thumb
one of our leading developers

Your suit is denied
but your letter will be published
to the editor, john fingers

Kafka

Who is that dude
who when things go wrong
always laughs

Who when things go right
smiles knowingly
He looks a lot like you

but not like you,
stern valedictorian
of the reaction

nor your accomplice
in the costume
of the coming revolution

Giant redwoods

A cross-section of the trunk has been marked
with a felt-tip pen to indicate
important historical coincidence

When drake sailed the main
When adam smith scribbled
When lumber went multi-national

and the shit hit the fan
When it hailed on the soccer match
and the exits were locked

happened after this one was felled
Later still I hit my hand
with the hammer and yelled

Reality, of continuing interest

The highway patrol often overestimate
the speed of a car painted red

Persons subject to leadfoot
often drive red-coloured cars

She wore white lipstick

Burn someone lightly with the tip
of your unexpected cigarette and listen
to the natural man like kierkegaard
advised you dig

Civ = blab

His arm fell off
The loss was noted

'Whatever has a heinie
has a mouth'

His arm went south
What stayed, voted

'The dolphins are trying to
communicate'

'Tell them to f██ off'

Ex catheter

Trespassing is not allowed at the river
Well tell us dickhead where it is permitted
Not along the homely guadalupe
Nor in city hall

do they listen to themselves
which same lack of attention
is directed at the landscape
that we note has us in it

Fiction of neutralized culture

Next he'll hit us with the pantheon of classicity
My discontented soul with the beauty it has lost
The new moon with the old moon in her arms
and there can be no compromise
We've had a belly-full of that

Seated at the organ (groan)
for robert grenier

The brain is bigger
than this figure
rapidly approaching

These days the students demand to be tested

The century is felt to be a single lifespan
Toward the end it wants to straighten out
Such debauches in those heedless decades!
So the superego is hoisted into the saddle
where it proceeds to go totally out of control

Or select a picture less pendulous
We need to get that piece of paper
as all the world begins to wave one
It simply hasn't been internalized yet
so we can't appear inner-directed

Song: Brilliantly inventive
for opal nations

Pomade upon the hair
and then the promenade
where the sun like orangeade
flickers off the waves
like lemonade and knocks
your knickers off for foreignaid
and kicks your knockers off

Feeling for the blind
for michael palmer

Being a superstitious person
accords wisdom to old ways
There's no control so who can say
Better safe than sorry
and not somehow mean it
We are nonetheless civilized
with a touching faith in reason
so a sense of contradiction
goes with me all my days
around ladders and over cracks
and when night comes
in dreams and violent rites
attacks the vacant space
while thinking twice

Vehicle

This little word
that once meant destiny
has a middle syllable
that's increased in intensity
until it sounds like a hiccup
but i don't think it means much

Manana from heaven

I just want a couple acres
in beautiful country
where I can put two-three chevys
up on cinder blocks
and abandon a stack
of automobile tires

One

The pain of that becoming many
who walk away creates dictators
who reduce variety to a monologue
concerning the uninterruptible
by its name of destiny
and then i shrug and go inside

Zither music

Straw wine bottles
Fishnet ceilings
Bits of driftwood
and the large glass
balls of nippon fisherfolk
to be a warning to us all

Associations

May not have much to do with thought
If you don't join them
they will come to you
If you do join
they will come in any case
so you have your fun
on other people's time
making many contacts
among whom was one
you probably don't remember

Open wide

The last time i went to the dentist
there was nowhere to spit
Not simply that they inserted the saliva-sucker
but once they took that thing back out
he saw me looking frantically around
'Cost accounting showed us each time a patient spits
we're losing time so we removed those bowls'
he told me as i swallowed to show i understood

The fate of presence in our time

might be the pbs equivalent
to these shots of the nuclear plant
where those accused and even more
importantly, their drugs
are nowhere to be seen
but we know they're there
somewhere inside these walls
inside the chainlink fence
inside that big box over there

The poet strolls at evening by the river
for tom sharp

You swing on the acacia boughs
over the chainlink fence
to scramble up the bank
and run across the freeway

then down the other side
and through that fence
you come at last to the railroad track
and next to that the creek
where your leisurely stroll at evening may commence

The referents' lair
for george bowering

Carter was talking to the shah
about a country which had blossomed forth
under enlightened leadership
About then i found what i was looking for
The weather and the sports reports

Soyez raisonnable

'Every bit of experience
comes like a voice from the past'
to make me sound like an idiot
in my objective advocations

like the city engineer
who's attached to his career
with its inbuilt biasses
to what's wisely termed growth

as in You should have that
surgically removed
Though it destroy the very realm
he'd never halt it

Thus i conclude that city engineers
or managers or planners
have a conflict of interest
about further developments

Don't drool when you say lot-split

How you feel about that meadow
personally will only
embarrass us

before the planning commission
The chair drums with his fingers
This is really irrelevant

He needs to see figures
not these shards of the pomo
These ghostly vernal pools

Nor even that the schools
are to the max or traffic
for these are merely

cumulative impact zones
possibly significant
Latin terms leave gringos cold
which is our preferred condition

Scum to sun

I'm really something only you
look down on, floating to the top
because so little substance
holds me down, i'm lighter

than whatever is beneath me,
and so it's me it sees
whenever it looks up and thinks
i am the light. And when the tank

empties, and what supported me
soaks back into the soil,
i'll be clinging to the sides
at my appointed level

Tubal legislature

The anchor-person is
acting. The president is
acting. The woman
taking a shower in the
commercial is nakedly
acting. The man
using his voice
to tell us what number
we should call is audibly
acting. The surprised
diplomat probably was
covertly acting. The burn
victim wishes that she
were acting. So does
the nurse.

Book ends

She liked a look of agony
while he would sooner help
another come — together
they languish in the simulacrum

wondering Are we
hungry or is it
only something
we just ate

Clearings in the throat
for anselm hollo

The grass has grown
over the old scythe

The cork in the wine
no-one would drink has crumbled

Closer to the graves
the paths grow clearer

Come out of hiding , despair
you're even shyer than joy

The poet

Society's the subject, you
the predicate. Call check
when you're to make that
presentation. Find those
citibank statements and read
the campus paper to be pleased
someone remembers the bismarck

Of course there's lots of ww 2 on pbs
Grainy corpses around stalingrad
who still perhaps believed
'I give my life for the fatherland
– i make a difference'
I for one enjoy arranging sounds
in the tradition of the text
whose need of tone
i respond to when alone
and happy, albeit sounding blue
not to be doing what i'm told to do

Clocks
for cecelia belle

circled future and past

Handled time

and spatialized the same

impulse become now

actuarial in

measureless presence

That's it for clocks
whose cuckoos, quirks and curlicues
introduce the decorative element
with the customary loss of striking power

Ancient riff

The beast in the forest
stands out among that beauty
and will repel
the driven decontextualist

O gorgeous ugliness
Please bear this message
to your serene mistress
of my severe uneasiness

Creation seems all one
save for your slobbermouth self
and me, come to reflect on it
How can she heal this breach

You must first let me hug you said the beast
So she believes you mean no harm
And then the ambience spoke out
I said nothing of the kind

Art as reven$\overset{u}{\cancel{g}}$*e*

Hear, me-you, here
your utterance is
authentic as anything

turned into print.
Cherished cat of the occident,
i who sprayed the sacred shrines

am shit-scared in the present
by people working for a living.
Thus i flatten you

into a piece of currency
prized among taste-makers
who select only for

the likes of we-we
and you-you. Definitely
not the shadow of a g

stretch ing out from
your feet (pause)
swearing he's beneath us

Might be right
for samuel brittan

Rawls' test of justice says
Pretend you're not born yet
so you might be born a millionaire
or you might be born a pauper
Now what social system do you choose

I saw myself sitting here saying this
with no small degree of smugness
assured of its success
I might be Rawls himself

for we share the same reason
except that a man began to shout
that he had a gun
We looked up then
It was an expensive one, more accurate

P.g., or, a canadian narrative
for barry mckinnon

Out one window snow
was visible, the other
gave onto a wonderland
modeled on tahiti and
crammed with families
come ten hours from the
hinterland to sit in
saunas and jacuzzis while
their kids on their spring
breaks do the giant water
slides. Worn out with
contradictions he slept
and dreamed his ex was
doing the nude hula to
some native drums but
waking, hears knocking as
room service cometh to
deliver an (albeit thin)
extra blanket he has asked
for and has, grudgingly,
belatedly, and now, been given

Meanwhile

There's this museum
where being hangs
by eternity and freedom
and you stand on line to enter
on your day off

And aren't they lovely
They're so human
Care, altruism and self-sacrifice
These knew how to paint
pictures that trap depth
as a mental sensation

Kant was right or ought to be
listened to, there's no-one here
but us on mondays when it's shut
and we remember
how we don't know what to do
about those who tell us what

to, since we need them and they
don't need us as we'd
really like to be, one at a time
while in a mob
it's impossible to see a thing
that isn't hung real high

Orphic

Have you found the entrance to the underworld
It's behind that ancient tree
Next to that impressive boulder
Within that dizzy chasm
Or over there maybe
under that clump of thistle
or one of these holes
dug by an apparently huge
colony of rabbits
Then there are the spaces in between
Harder to identify because apparently unmarked
You maybe ought to check there too

Trance ending

Classical music
I've said it before
moves me to the truth

of feelings more objective
than i had before it played
It is of use

in the vending of expensive foreign goods
The indigent stand up when it is heard
and we cry when objects penetrate our hide

Male order brides
for michael davidson

Men give the months girls' names
then pin them over their garbage.
And on their calendars
these words appear:
Steve's Auto Body Shop
above a closeup of some gorgeous
big blossoms.

But the heart would be accurate.
It hates the head for saying
Heart, i know you hate me.
For getting there ahead of itself
and ruining the landscape (those
mounds and brush-choked hollows).

All that's vague, sketched-in,
suggestive
wants to stroke him
till his skin
fits. But the heart

tired of having what it heard
it wanted, hates it.
For it's a long, long time

And the heart
Its only analogy

(Rimes with January
from Janus
who gathers
and who hunts
the question
we paste upon
its answer

Voice

Voracious
orifice
i
can't
express

Prophetic soul mode

The sweep of his assertions
put me in mind of sussex england
where with my father the filmmaker
as a lad i watched and wondered
as the model (anthony
steel, later to be famous
briefly as anita ekberg's
mate) in shorts and singlet
sprinted over the down
into the crotch of a wood
shaped like a v
over and over until it was right
and a wrap but when
i saw the movie he was so tiny
he could have been anyone
or even me

Da capo

Dim, mousy, nervous
sullen, jealous, and
resentful (as
reported) woman

The problem as identified
by the husband (somewhat
suave) who (as his wife
asserts) has his stuff together

and seems the credible
half of this distressing
dyad (in the flick
he poisons her)

with a high-powered business
woman in new york to which
he frequently repairs
He has admitted the affair

to his wife who knows, just
knows, the other is
beautiful and smart
and sane, her hubby says so

So the therapist suggests
he bring her picture in
so they can talk
about it next time: dim

Good god! you, here?

Given non-referential art
can account for itself
in old-fangled prose

and this cup is empty
since once it was full

it's not so much politics
or economics as aesthetics

Given clear thinking
is no more a chimera
than some other sort

in a time of missing links
then won't one startle
at a long-forgotten fence
or face

Obligatory poem of the perspicacious child
for robert creeley

She's learned a new word
Now she sees a lot of holes

On going on
for cydney chadwick

The powers-that-be
are represented by
a roped-off rectangle

where the hoi polloi
may drink and dance
and even laugh for free.

I'm bored. Toronto,
nyc, london, paree —
even god's own country:

i keep recurring
to that design.
And *i* can't mean *me*

Personal (1)

The queen of the night
has a startling aria
in the language of opera

The person known as suzanne
scarcely more than a child
in the language of biography

in the temple of iconography
was mistaken
for the object of a quest

A woman with the tail of an ocelot
of whom one had learned
at his mother's so-called knee

Personal (too)

She bent to read the same page he read
Heat radiated from therefore her body
The book was called (she said)
Civilization and its discotheques
and life was too short to complete it

So, a poetry of immediacy

Nothing happens that is not the mind
to us, this side of Ouch

It can be argued that resistance
is of another order
absent here

by those who don't see the alternatives
zooming past like sideroads

but not by those who think
the immediate is
Shit, i just ran out of paper

Confidence

All that counts, artists
have it in their art
or they're not artists

But the mad flaunt it as well
and the wealthy born to wealth

A few hundred remote tribespersons
their homelands being razed

Some sportspersons and other gamblers
and lovers
half the time
with 50% justification
where i asserted
he asserts

But one dimension

H von h remarked
Break open evening
(the word) to feel
thick flowing meaning

All words are pleasure
To have some complaint
ensures their generation
and should make one grateful

And we do have some complaint

Where we came in

Tiny courts — he dead
Scales now fallen
from said eyes
onto our shoulders
where our heads

resume the burden
laid again
by blind faith
out of the individual
vision

Well i've seen the world
20-20 once upon a time
It's left me here
far-sighted

Take me back
to saskatchewan
moans the train
that then ran

to the quest it began

David Bromige grew up in England. He lived for a time in Saskatchewan, Ontario, Alberta and British Columbia where, in the early 1960s, he was at university with members of the coalescing TISH group, sharing their interest in the poetics of Olson, Creeley and Duncan. After moving to Berkeley, and publishing his early books with Black Sparrow Press, he became, with his work *Tight Corners,* in the words of Ron Silliman, 'the first to open up the question [in poetry] of language's cognitive domain'. While the extension of this project in such books as *My Poetry, P-E-A-C-E* and *Red Hats* has allied him with the $L=A=N=G=U-A=G=E$ writers, his 1988 selected poems, *Desire,* which won him the Western States Arts Federation Award, reveals a range no rubric can subsume. He has published books in the UK, the USA, and Canada, and remains a Canadian citizen, notwithstanding his long-time residence in California, where since 1970 he has taught at Sonoma State University.